EARTH'S CONTINENTS

Antarctica

by Mary Lindeen

Antarctica is the **continent** on the most southern part of Earth. The **South Pole** is in the middle of Antarctica.

Arctic Ocean

EUROPE

ASIA

NORTH
AMERICA

Atlantic
Ocean

AFRICA

Pacific
Ocean

Pacific
Ocean

SOUTH
AMERICA

Indian

Ocean

Atlantic
Ocean

AUSTRALIA

N

W   E

S

ANTARCTICA

Antarctica is one of seven continents on Earth.

The Pacific, Atlantic, and Indian Oceans come together around Antarctica. Some people call this the Southern Ocean. Giant **icebergs** float near the continent's shores.

Most of an iceberg is underwater. Only the top shows above water.

Almost all of Antarctica is covered by ice. But there are some bare, rocky areas. These are mostly on top of the mountains.

*Say it! *jen-TOO*

Gentoo* penguins build their nests on ice-free shores.

Antarctica holds most of the ice and **fresh water** on Earth. It also has the coldest temperatures in the world.

The ice in Antarctica makes up more than half of all fresh water on Earth.

The middle of Antarctica is very dry. It almost never snows there. Instead, the wind blows snow in from other areas.

Most of Antarctica is empty.

Not many plants or animals live on Antarctica's land areas. Most of the animals live in the ocean. Most of the plants are very small.

This young Antarctic fur seal lives near the ocean.

No people live in Antarctica. But **scientists** stay there for months at a time to study the continent.

Scientists live at special **science stations** while they work.

The scientists have all of their supplies brought in by ship or by air. They are careful to protect themselves from the cold.

Special ships cut through the ice to bring supplies to scientists.

Some **countries** say that parts of Antarctica belong to them. Other people think that the world needs to share this continent.

Many countries have science stations in Antarctica. They share the space.

Would you like to be a scientist in Antarctica? Maybe someday you will see Antarctica for yourself!

Emperor penguins live in Antarctica.

Glossary

continent (KON-tuh-nent): A continent is one of seven large land areas on Earth. Antarctica is a continent.

countries (KUN-trees): Countries are areas of land with their own governments. Many countries believe parts of Antarctica belong to them.

fresh water (FRESH WAH-tur): Fresh water is water that does not contain salt. It is found in most lakes and rivers. If Antarctica's ice melted it would be fresh water.

icebergs (EYESS-bergs): Icebergs are large chunks of ice that float in the ocean. Icebergs can be found off the coast of Antarctica.

science stations (SYE-uhnss STAY-shuhns): Science stations are places where people study and do experiments. Scientists who go to Antarctica study in science stations.

scientists (SYE-uhn-tists): Scientists are people who study the world by testing, experimenting, and measuring. Scientists visit Antarctica to study the land and animals.

South Pole (SOWTH POHL): The South Pole is the most southern point on Earth. The South Pole is in Antarctica.

To Find Out More

Books

Fowler, Allan. *Antarctica*. Danbury, CT: Children's Press, 2001.

Hooper, Meredith, and Lucia deLeiris. *Antarctic Journal: The Hidden Worlds of Antarctica's Animals*. London: Frances Lincoln Publishers, 2001.

Sayre, April Pulley. *Hooray For Antarctica!* Brookfield, CT: Millbrook Press, 2003.

Web Sites

Visit our Web site for links about Antarctica: *childsworld.com/links*

Note to Parents, Teachers, and Librarians: We routinely verify our Web links to make sure they are safe and active sites. So encourage your readers to check them out!

Index

About the Author

Mary Lindeen is an elementary school teacher who turned her love of children and books into a career in publishing. She has written and edited many library books and literacy programs. She also enjoys traveling with her son, Benjamin, whenever and wherever she can.

On the cover: There are many interesting ice shapes in Antarctica.

Published by The Child's World®
1980 Lookout Drive • Mankato, MN 56003-1705
800-599-READ • www.childsworld.com

ACKNOWLEDGMENTS
The Child's World®: Mary Berendes, Publishing Director
The Design Lab: Design, page, and map production
Red Line Editorial: Editorial direction

PHOTO CREDITS: iStockphoto, cover; Stephen Coburn/Shutterstock Images, 5; Gary Yim/Shutterstock Images, 7; Armin Rose/ Shutterstock Images, 9, 11; Alexander Hafemann/iStockphoto, 13; Steve Estvanik/iStockphoto, 15; Andrey Pavlov/iStockphoto, 17; Steve Estvanik/123rf, 19; Gentoo Multimedia Ltd./Shutterstock Images, 21

Printed in the United States of America in Mankato, Minnesota.
November 2009
F11460

LIBRARY OF CONGRESS CATALOGING-IN-PUBLICATION DATA
Lindeen, Mary.
 Antarctica / by Mary Lindeen.
   p. cm. — (Earth's continents)
 Includes index.
 ISBN 978-1-60253-347-9 (library bound : alk. paper)
 1. Antarctica—Juvenile literature. I. Title. II. Series.
 G863.L56 2010
 919.8'9—dc22   2009030018